C000094143

Anglic Ordination Rites

The Berkeley Statement: 'To Equip the Saints'

Findings of the Sixth International
Anglican Liturgical Consultation,
Berkeley, California, 2001

Edited by Paul Gibson

Coordinator for Liturgy for the
Anglican Consultative Council

GROVE BOOKS LIMITED
RIDLEY HALL RD CAMBRIDGE CB3 9HU

Contents

The Cover Illustration is the Compassrose, the symbol of the Anglican Communion

Copyright © The Secretary General of the Anglican Consultative Council 2002

First Impression February 2002
ISSN 0144-1728
ISBN 1 85174 489 4

Introduction

In 1991 the International Anglican Liturgical Consultation met in Toronto, Canada, and produced a statement on Christian Initiation.[1] This was intended to be the first of three statements in response to the 1982 report of the Faith and Order Commission of the World Council of Churches, *Baptism, Eucharist and Ministry* (commonly called the Lima Report).[2]

In 1993 an interim conference was held in Untermarchtal, Germany, and the results published in *Revising the Eucharist: Groundwork for the Anglican Communion*.[3] Then the full International Consultation met in Dublin, Ireland, in 1995 and produced the second Statement, this time on the Eucharist.[4]

To begin work in the area of ordination, a preparatory conference was again held, this time in Järvenpää, Finland, in 1997. The preparatory papers were published later that year as *Anglican Orders and Ordinations*.[5] The Consultation intended to conclude the work on Ordination was called in 1999 in Kottayam, Kerala, India, but had to be abandoned because of difficulties with the Indian government. At least twelve participants were denied entry visas and those who did arrive were forbidden to meet formally. However, much informal work was completed in India and handed on to the Steering Committee to continue the process of developing the statement further. A draft statement was presented to those who gathered at the Church Divinity School of the Pacific in Berkeley, California, USA, in August 2001.

Thirty of the thirty-seven Anglican Provinces were represented at Berkeley, together with a participant from the Mar Thoma Church, providing the widest representation of the Communion at an IALC thus far. Participants worked together for the best part of a week and the attached statement is the result of their labours. The statement covers the areas of the theology of ordination and the liturgies of ordination. It represents a very wide consensus among liturgists of our Communion. Other related topics were raised for future discussion, including discernment, preparation and formation for ordination, renewal of ordination promises, and celebration of new ministry.

The attached statement is offered to the Churches of the Anglican Communion for study, and it is hoped that it will be of use to those Provinces engaged in revision of ordination liturgies, now or in the future.

Ronald L Dowling (Chair of IALC, 1995–2001)

---

1   David R Holeton (ed), *Christian Initiation in the Anglican Communion: The Toronto Statement 'Walk in Newness of Life'* (Grove Worship booklet W 118).
2   *Baptism, Eucharist and Ministry* (Faith and Order Paper No 111, WCC, Geneva, 1982)—'BEM.'
3   David R Holeton, (ed), *Revising the Eucharist: Groundwork for the Anglican Communion* (Alcuin/GROW Joint Liturgical Study JLS 27).
4   David R Holeton (ed), *Renewing the Anglican Eucharist* (Grove Worship booklet W 135).
5   David R Holeton (ed), *Anglican Orders and Ordinations* (Alcuin/GROW Joint Liturgical Study JLS 39).

1

The Ordered Nature of the Church

The Calling of the People of God

The whole of creation is called into being through the abundant love of God, who in Christ participates in the world's life so that we may share in the triune life of love and joy. Through the Holy Spirit God baptizes us into the life and ministry of Christ and forms us into the *laos*, the people of God, who as signs and agents of God's reign participate in God's mission of reconciling humanity and all creation to God. This is the *ecclesia*, the church, the new community called into being by God.

The foundation of the life and ministry of the church is therefore baptism.[6] As Jesus' ministry was inaugurated by baptism, so in our baptism into the life of Christ we are anointed by the Holy Spirit 'to bring good news to the poor...to proclaim release to the captives and recovery of sight to the blind, to let the oppressed go free, to proclaim the year of the Lord's favour' (Luke 4.18–19). In baptism, the people of God are revealed to be a holy people (1 Peter 2.9–10), ministering to the world in the name and in the manner of Christ.

Baptism and Ministry

God bestows upon the church a variety of gifts to build up the body of Christ and to participate in God's mission in the world.[7] Within the Spirit-filled body, different charisms are given by God to every member, including prophecy, evangelism, teaching, healing, discernment, wisdom, administration and leadership (Romans 12.4–8, 1 Corinthians 12.4–12).

In order that the whole people of God may fulfill their calling to be a holy priesthood, serving the world by ministering Christ's reconciling love in the power of the Spirit, some are called to specific ministries of leadership by ordination. Although the New Testament refers to a number of different ministries of leadership (see Ephesians 4.11–12, 1 Timothy 3.1–13, 1 Peter 5.1–5), by the second century the ordering of bishops, presbyters, and deacons emerged within the wider context of the ministry of the whole church.

Over the course of Christian history, there have been various understandings of the relationship between the people of God (the *laos*) and ordained

---

6 Beginning our theology of ministry with the baptismal ministry of the whole people of God has significant implications for ecumenical dialogue. Provinces are urged to consider this baptismal perspective in their ecumenical discussions.

7 'The complementary gifts bestowed by the Holy Spirit in the community are for the common good and for the building up of the church and for the service of the world to which the church is sent' (*Virginia Report* 3.20).

ministers. In some times and places, ordination was viewed as conferring a status elevating ordained ministers above the laity. However, understanding baptism as the foundation of the life and ministry of the church (that is, having a baptismal ecclesiology) leads us to see ordained ministers as integral members of the body of Christ, called by God and discerned by the body to be signs and animators of Christ's self-giving life and ministry to which all people are called by God and for which we are empowered by the Spirit.

Cultural Shaping of Ministry

The ways in which the church develops its theology, orders its life for mission, and takes up the threefold ordering of ministry interact with various aspects of our cultures. Cultures involve social styles, conceptual and material symbols, the technologies that sustain life, and languages, the arts, and other media of communication. They include the way people are present to themselves and to each other in community, as well as the ways in which leaders emerge, are acknowledged, and exercise their relationships and roles within communities.[8]

The gospel both affirms and challenges these cultural expressions of relationships and leadership. The historic threefold ordering of ministry will be embodied in different manners in various parts of the Anglican Communion, but ordained ministry must always be in service of the ministry of the whole people of God. The task of discerning which aspects of the culture offer patterns of leadership and ritual celebration that enable ordained ministers to serve the people of God belongs to the people of that culture. This work of inculturation is always carried out in faithfulness to the baptismal call to participate in Christ's ministry.[9]

Bishops

God bestows upon the church the ministry of oversight (*episcope*) which historically found its focus in the office of the bishop. As the one called by the baptized community for a ministry of oversight, the bishop is the sign of unity and of continuity with the apostolic tradition of faith and life. In the liturgical role, 'the bishop expresses the unity of the church by presiding at its liturgical rites. Whenever possible, the bishop presides at baptism, whether of adults or children, and eucharist, leading the people in offering the sacrifice of praise and thanksgiving.'[10] The role of the bishop is summed up in this way in the *Virginia Report* of the Inter-Anglican Theological and Doctrinal Commission: 'The calling of a bishop is to represent Christ and his church,

---

8 Structures of decision-making and styles of leadership in the church often reflect, at least to some extent, the parallel structures of society.
9 For further discussion, see *Anglican Orders and Ordinations* (JLS 39) pp 52ff.
10 *Walk in Newness of Life* 3.39 (Grove Worship booklet W 118).

particularly as apostle, chief priest, teacher and pastor of a diocese; to guard the faith, unity and discipline of the whole church; to proclaim the word of God; to act in Christ's name for the reconciliation of the world and the building up of the church; and to ordain others to continue Christ's ministry.'[11] Pastoral oversight involves humble self-offering on behalf of others, rooted in the ministry of Christ, who as good shepherd lays down his life for his people. Thus episcopacy is exercised as a service to the community, a ministry that is intended to build up the whole people of God.

In reflecting on the role of the episcopate, it is important to consider the historical, cultural and social contexts in which the episcopal office has developed. In the pre-Nicene period, the church was seen as a sub-culture within the wider society. The bishop was teacher and pastor and the bond of communion both within the local church and between the various local and regional churches. Bishops also exercised a ministry of prophetic witness. In the period after Constantine, the role of the bishop changed significantly. The bishop became part of the hierarchical administrative structure of the empire on the model of the imperial civil service. In the feudal period in the West the bishop was both spiritual and temporal lord. After the Reformation in England the relationship between church and state characteristic of the Constantinian era did not fundamentally change. The imperial and feudal models of episcopacy continued to predominate in the Church of England, and the episcopate functioned culturally and sociologically as part of the civil establishment. As Anglicanism spread around the globe, it was this style of episcopacy which tended to predominate during the period of colonialism. This model, however, was not universal, and in some places it was modified by an increased sense of the role played by the bishop in leading the mission of the church and by a heightened emphasis on the apostolic nature of the episcopate.

In the Anglican Communion today, a renewed model of episcopal leadership is emerging, one that more fully reflects the servant ministry of Jesus and the baptismal calling of the whole people of God. In this style of episcopal leadership, the ministries of all the baptized are nurtured in ways which are personal, collegial, and communal.[12] 'Every diocese in the Anglican Communion knows something of the exercise of the personal ministry of oversight of the bishop (or bishops); of collegiality in the coming together of bishops and clergy; and of the communal dimension of oversight which brings together the bishop with clergy and laity in the meeting of synods. These dimensions of the ministry of oversight are expressed in different ways in the different regions of the world and are affected by local circumstance

---

11 *The Virginia Report: The Report of the Inter-Anglican Theological and Doctrinal Commission*, 3.17.
12 See *BEM*, 'Ministry' 26.

and custom.'[13]

This vision of the episcopate ought to find expression in the ordination rite for bishops and in the way in which episcopal ministry is exercised both within the local diocese and in the collegial oversight which the episcopate exercises regionally and internationally. For example, the ordination of a bishop should affirm and celebrate the ministry of the bishop in and among the members of the Spirit-filled community in which the bishop has been called to exercise oversight. In a similar fashion, the seating of the bishop should be a sign of the bishop's role as chief pastor and teacher of the community rather than an enthronement reminiscent of the imperial model. The bishop's leadership will foster a dynamic relationship among the parishes of the diocese grounded in the organic unity of the baptismal community with its diversity of gifts and ministries, including the ordained ministries of presbyter and deacon.

Presbyters/Priests

The calling of presbyters is 'to share with the bishops in the overseeing of the church.'[14] Just as the ministry of the bishop is rooted in Christ's self-offering, so also the ministry of the presbyter is offered in service of the whole people of God. The presbyter's distinctive pastoral and spiritual ministry in the community is expressed particularly in proclaiming the word and presiding at baptism and eucharist. 'Presbyters serve as pastoral ministers of word and sacraments in a local eucharistic community. They are preachers and teachers of the faith, exercise pastoral care, and bear responsibility for the discipline of the congregation to the end that the world may believe and that the entire membership of the church may be renewed, strengthened and equipped in ministry. Presbyters have particular responsibility for the preparation of members for Christian life and ministry.'[15] As the bishop's representative in the local community, a distinctive feature of the presbyter's ministry is to identify and nurture the gifts of the Spirit given to the community for the work of ministry.

The New Testament uses the term *presbyteros* in reference to the 'elders' of Christian communities (Acts 15.4–6; 20.17), and the language of priesthood to speak of Christ (Hebrews 4.14–5.10) and of the whole community of the baptized (1 Peter 2.4–5; Revelation 1.6). When applied to Christ, priestly language refers to the sacrificial nature of his death (Hebrews 7.26–28) and to Christ's intercession before God on behalf of all creation (Hebrews 7.23–25; Romans 8.34). When applied to all the baptized, priestly language refers to the 'living sacrifice, holy and acceptable to God' (Romans 12.1) which

---

13   *Virginia Report* 3.22
14   *Virginia Report* 3.18
15   *BEM*, 'Ministry' 30.

7

they offer. As the ordained ministry developed, language of priesthood became increasingly applied first to the office of bishop and then derivatively to the presbyterate, and sacrificial and vicarial interpretations of this ministry were overlaid upon the earlier presbyteral understanding. At the time of the Reformation, the Anglican ordinal retained the term 'priest,' interpreting this office as one in which the minister unites the proclamation of the word, the administration of the sacraments, and the pastoral care of the community.

In the various languages used in the Anglican Communion today, different terms are used for the office, with different connotations arising from historical, cultural, and linguistic factors. Provinces that use the term 'priest' (or a translation thereof) may be guided by the interpretation of the term in *Baptism, Eucharist and Ministry*: 'Ordained ministers are related, as are all Christians, both to the priesthood of Christ, and to the priesthood of the church. But they may appropriately be called priests because they fulfill a particular priestly service by strengthening and building up the royal and prophetic priesthood of the faithful through word and sacraments, through their prayers of intercession, and through their pastoral guidance of the community.'[16] For example, priests/presbyters are appointed to declare God's forgiveness and announce God's blessing in order that the whole priestly people of God may be witnesses of reconciliation and agents of blessing in the world.

Whichever term is used, ordination rites should make use of a wide range of imagery in order to bring out the multi-faceted meaning of this office. Consistent with a baptismal ecclesiology, the ordination rite should affirm the priesthood of the baptized community and the sacramental, pastoral and teaching relationship of the presbyter to the entire community.

Deacons

In the Anglican Communion today, there are various experiences and understandings of the diaconate, not only from province to province but even within provinces. It is important to learn from one another and to be sensitive to the different needs and cultural contexts in different parts of the Communion.

Historically, deacons were often managers of the local church, holding considerable authority. They also oversaw the charitable and social work of the church. The practical and the liturgical dimensions developed hand in hand and reflected each other. During the Middle Ages, the diaconate became principally a transitional order on the way to the presbyterate, and at the time of the Reformation the Church of England retained this practice.

In some places, the diaconate is being renewed as a distinct office, drawing upon New Testament (*eg* Acts 6.1–6) and patristic evidence of the serv-

16   *BEM*, 'Ministry' 17.

ant ministry of deacons. In this renewed understanding, the ministry of the deacon is primarily directed towards the servant mission of the church in the world and has as one of its principal aims 'to interpret to the church the needs, concerns, and hopes of the world.'[17] The liturgical role of the deacon expresses this interface between the world and the baptismal community.

Although it is sometimes asserted today that the diaconate is the basis for the servant character of all three orders, it is baptism into the life of Christ which is the basis for the servant character of all the church's ministries. The distinctive nature of the diaconate is not servant ministry in itself, but the calling of deacons to be signs and animators of the Christ-like service of the whole people of God in the world. Both the missionary, world-directed aspect and the liturgical aspect of the diaconal ministry ought to find expression in the ordination rite for deacons.

Direct Ordination

Because the three orders are viewed as distinct ministries, direct ordination to the presbyterate, and even the possibility of direct ordination to the episcopate, are being advocated by some in the Anglican Communion. There is historical precedent for both sequential and direct ordination. In the pre-Nicene church, direct ordination was commonly practised, and sequential ordination did not become universal until the eleventh century. Provinces may therefore wish to consider the possibility of direct ordination to the episcopate and to the presbyterate.

The Act of Ordination

The act of ordination is the liturgical expression of the church's appointment of its ministers. In the ecumenical document *Baptism, Eucharist and Ministry* the meaning of ordination is expressed in a way which is consistent with an Anglican understanding of ordination:

'Ordination denotes an action by God and the community by which the ordained are strengthened by the Spirit for their task and are upheld by the acknowledgment and prayers of the congregation.

A long and early Christian tradition places ordination in the context of worship and especially of the eucharist. Such a place for the service of ordination preserves the understanding of ordination as an act of the whole community, and not of a certain order within it or of the individual ordained. The act of ordination by the laying on of hands of those appointed to do so is at one and the same time invocation of the Holy Spirit (*epiklesis*); sacramental sign; acknowledgment of gifts and commitment.

---

17 From 'The Ordination of a Deacon' in *The Book of Alternative Services of the Anglican Church of Canada*, p 655.

(a) Ordination is an invocation to God that the new minister be given the power of the Holy Spirit in the new relation which is established between this minister and the local Christian community and, by intention, the church universal. The otherness of God's initiative, of which the ordained ministry is a sign, is here acknowledged in the act of ordination itself. 'The Spirit blows where it wills' (John 3.3): the invocation of the Spirit implies the absolute dependence on God for the outcome of the church's prayer. This means that the Spirit may set new forces in motion and open new possibilities 'far more abundantly than all that we ask or think' (Eph 3.20).

(b) Ordination is a sign of the granting of this prayer by the Lord who gives the gift of the ordained ministry. Although the outcome of the church's *epiklesis* depends on the freedom of God, the church ordains in confidence that God, being faithful to his promise in Christ, enters sacramentally into contingent, historical forms of human relationship and uses these for his purpose. Ordination is a sign performed in faith that the spiritual relationship signified is present in, with and through the words spoken, the gestures made and the forms employed.

(c) Ordination is an acknowledgment by the church of the gifts of the Spirit in the one ordained, and a commitment by both the church and the ordinand to the new relationship. By receiving the new minister in the act of ordination, the congregation acknowledges the minister's gifts and commits itself to be open towards these gifts. Likewise those ordained offer their gifts to the church and commit themselves to the burden and opportunity of new authority and responsibility. At the same time, they enter into a collegial relationship with other ordained ministers.'[18]

This understanding of ordination reflects a baptismal ecclesiology. It is the community as a whole, with the bishop presiding, which recognizes the divine call and the gifts of ministry of those who are to be ordained. It is the community as a whole which through prayer with the laying on of hands by the bishop as the focus of the church's unity seeks from God the necessary increase of those gifts and graces for the effective exercise of the ministry. It is the community as a whole which authorizes and sends forth the ordained in God's name to lead the baptized in Christ's mission and ministry. All of these dimensions of ordination ought to find expression in the rite.

18 *BEM*, 'Ministry' 40–44.

2
The Liturgy of Ordination

A. General Principles

1. Christian baptism implies a commitment to serve God through the church in and for the world. It is thus the foundation for Christian ministry, both of the church as a whole, and of each of its members, including those called to serve Jesus Christ as bishops, presbyters, or deacons. Setting ordination rites in such a theological context is an expression of what is meant by a 'baptismal ecclesiology.'

2. Ordination rites should be grounded in a baptismal ecclesiology, not only in setting ordination to particular ministries firmly within the context of the ministry of the whole people of God, but also in demonstrating the principle (from the Dublin Statement) that 'in, through and with Christ, the assembly is the celebrant…'[19]

3. An ordination service is an ecclesial event in which the church's life and ministry is ordered, and so should take place in the context of a eucharist celebrated at a place and time when all its ministries may be most fully represented. (The eucharistic structure outlined in the Dublin Statement provides a sound basis within which ordination to each order may take place, during the prayer of the people of God, the 'royal priesthood').

4. The incarnational nature of the gospel calls Christians to embrace in their liturgy aspects of local culture that embody the values of the kingdom of God. Such things as dress, language and symbol in ordination rites all shape the way in which participants perceive the nature and significance of ministry, and how it is authorized and imparted (see the York Statement).[20]

5. Amid the great diversity of cultural expressions of ordination rites throughout the Communion, (a) the recognition by the church of God's call of the candidates and (b) prayer with the laying on of hands remain the central focus of the ordination rite.

6. The distinct character of each of the three ministries should be made clear. This is best seen when there is ordination to one order alone at any particular service, but all orders are represented in fulfilling their proper ministries within that service.

7. An ordination service is sometimes suggested as a suitable occasion when

---

19 *International Anglican Liturgical Consultation on the Eucharist, Dublin, 1995,* Principles and Recommen-·dations 2. See footnote 4 on page 3 above, or David R Holeton (ed), *Our Thanks and Praise: The Eucharist in Anglicanism Today* (Anglican Book Centre, Toronto, 1998) p 261.

20 See 'Down to Earth Worship' in David R Holeton (ed) *Liturgical Inculturation in the Anglican Communion* (Alcuin/GROW Joint Liturgical Study JLS 15).

other clergy or authorized lay ministers may be licensed. Such a practice tends to confuse ordination and licensing, may detract from the significance of the service for the ordinands, and may be in danger of appearing to express a clericalized understanding of the ministry of the *laos*, the people of God.

The above basic principles and the commentary which follows seek to set out the main elements and coherent guidelines for common patterns for ordination rites throughout the Communion, which Provinces can use according to their various cultural contexts.

B. Elements of the Rite
The Gathering of God's People

Setting ordination in the context of baptismal ecclesiology affects the service throughout. Yet the opening moments of any liturgical celebration greatly influence the way in which the entire rite will be understood by all the participants.

There are many possibilities for the gathering rite. It should not be seen as a mere preliminary to the act of ordination, but convey the sense that the whole church is coming together to order its life for ministry through ordaining some candidates in response to God's call given through that church. A fairly brief dialogue between bishop and people could constitute the assembly for this purpose, setting the context by celebrating the ministerial gifts of the whole church (see Eph 4.11–13), or the reaffirmation of baptismal faith (see below) might be used here.

The opening part of the service may also give recognition to the diverse relationships of the various members of the congregation both to the candidates and to the wider church (Anglican and ecumenical).

Regardless of how the candidates enter the building, they should be seated with those with whom they are closely linked, such as their family, those who have nurtured them in the community of faith, those who will present them for ordination, or those among whom they will serve. Care should be taken to ensure that the ordinands continue to sit with this supportive group until they are called forward for the Questions (see below).

The Presentation of the Candidates

The Presentation may appropriately take place within the Gathering so that the ordinands may be introduced to the community at the outset, or alternatively after the sermon, where it could also be set in the context of the reaffirmation of baptismal faith by the whole assembly and the continuing examination of the candidates (see below).

Provinces may consider the respective advantages and disadvantages of the Presentation of the candidates taking place at the door, at the font, or at a central visible place.

The particular process through which candidates have come to ordination ought to determine who will present them. For example, in some cases they may be presented by those who have discerned and nurtured the individual's call to—and preparation for—ordained ministry; in others it may be representatives of the local church among whom the new ministry is to be exercised. While the role played by family and friends may rightly be recognized at some point within an ordination service, the presenters should represent the wider community of the baptized rather than the personal choice of the candidate.

During the Presentation the presenters should affirm the candidate's call and readiness for this new and particular ordained ministry. A question concerning calling should follow and be answered by each candidate individually.

Sometimes the candidates—or others on their behalf—may tell their story, providing informal personal testimony about their experience of vocation, but in some cultures it is usually easier for personal information to be conveyed in other ways (for example, printed out or spoken about at the end or after the service).

Proclaiming and Receiving the Word of God

The liturgy of the word is a standard element in every Christian assembly. The ecclesial nature of ordination may be underscored if the eucharistic readings of the day are used, when they are appropriate, rather than those that focus more narrowly on the particular order being conferred.

The sermon should be an exposition of the word of God which has been read, in relation to the ministry of the whole church, and not be an address solely to the candidates, which belongs rather to a (set) Exhortation given by the bishop elsewhere in the rite.

Reaffirmation of Baptismal Faith

A reaffirmation of baptismal faith could be a significant feature of the rite, enabling the assembly to reaffirm God's call and its response to ministry. It is well suited to take place following the ministry of the word, as a foundation for the examination of the candidates, and leading to the ordination prayer. Such a position is akin to its equivalent place in many rites of baptism. (By 'reaffirmation of baptismal faith' is meant declarations of faith and repentance through recitation of the Apostles' Creed, perhaps in threefold responsive form, and expressions of commitment to a Christian lifestyle and ministry, both personal and corporate). The bishop's invitation to all Christians present to engage in this reaffirmation may well include material which is currently part of the Exhortation to candidates in most provinces.

Exhortation and Questions

The Exhortation and Questions may be divided into sections, so that some introductory statement about ordination and preliminary questions may form part of the Presentation; the main exhortation and central examination may take place after hearing God's word; and questions about the mission of the newly ordained and the 'sending forth' of them may be placed at the end of the service. Alternatively, all of these may be combined together in the centre of the rite.

The questions put to the candidates should focus on the specific qualities and duties required of the particular order.

This is the appropriate point, after the people have heard the candidates' answers and expression of commitment, for the bishop to ask the people if it is their will that the candidates be ordained and for them to affirm their commitment to support the candidates in their ministries. Rites which include an opportunity for the people to object to candidates should also allow for such an affirmation.

Prayer with the Laying on of Hands

Ordination prayer involves the prayer of the whole community. This raises the question as to how continuity between the prayer of all the faithful and the presidential prayer with the laying on of hands may be best achieved. Should the prayer of all the faithful be in silence or in the form of prayers of intercession led by a deacon or lay person—or both? If the second, then it should be a responsive form but not necessarily a standard litany, and whatever form is chosen should contain petitions for the ministry of the whole people of God, as well as prayers for the world, for peace, justice, reconciliation and creation. A hymn or song invoking the Holy Spirit and musical settings of any litany should be suitable for singing by the whole assembly.

The presidential ordination prayer should set thanksgiving for God's call of the ordinands to their particular ministry within the context of praise for the diversity of ministries given to the church by the Holy Spirit, and should make petition for the bestowal of the gifts and graces necessary for the effective exercise of that ministry. It might well be punctuated by appropriate congregational responses, and should culminate with a great 'Amen.'

The particular posture adopted by those involved—both the community offering prayer and those for whom the prayer is being offered—is significant. For example:

- if the bishop adopts the same posture as the rest of the assembly for the intercessory prayer and invocation of the Holy Spirit, the bishop is identified as praying with the whole community;
- if the candidates kneel while others stand, it is more clearly indicated that they are being prayed for;

- if both the presider and assembly stand for the presidential prayer, it is clearer that the act is that of the whole assembly and not just of the president alone;
- if those who are associated with the presidential imposition of hands (*ie*, presbyters at the ordination of presbyters, and bishops at episcopal ordinations) join in any other manual gestures with the president throughout the entire prayer, its unity is more clearly demonstrated.

Traditional Anglican ordination rites have located the laying on of hands after prayer and accompanied it with an imperative formula. Recent revisions have tended to revert to the more ancient custom of locating it during the presidential prayer itself. While this appropriately brings the two into closer association with one another, it raises problems when more than one candidate is to be ordained. Three options for the imposition of hands suggest themselves:

- before the prayer, in silence;
- during the epicletic (petitionary) section of the prayer, with part of it being repeated over each candidate (it is desirable for this to be a substantial portion of the section to avoid the impression that ordination is effected by a particular formula alone);
- at the end of the presidential prayer, in silence, before the doxology.

The ancient practice of the church seems to have been that usually the bishop alone laid on hands, and this continues to be the normal practice in most Eastern churches and at the ordination of a deacon in the West. In the Western tradition, however, it came to be the custom for presbyters at the ordination of presbyters, and bishops at the ordination of bishops, to join the president in laying on of hands. Nevertheless, not every one of the bishops or presbyters present needs to join in tactile contact for every candidate; the stretching out of the hands will suffice to associate others with the action and thereby help make the imposition of hands more visible to the rest of the congregation. It is also important that the way in which bishop, ordinands, and others move to and from the hand-laying should not by fussiness detract from the central act, nor should it destroy the unity of the presidential prayer.

In rites where the laying on of hands has been brought within the presidential prayer, it would be more consistent for the bishop to stand (without mitre) throughout the prayer, including the laying on of hands, rather than sit to lay on hands, as is sometimes the custom in traditional Anglican ordination rites.

Traditionally in Anglican rites the Bible has been given to those who are newly ordained immediately after the laying on of hands. However, because the ceremony fits naturally into the sending out of the newly ordained, serious consideration should be given to transferring this action to the final part of the service along with the presentation of any other secondary symbols of office. This would also help to preserve the centrality of the act of the laying on of hands, which should not be obscured by other symbolic actions, however generous and significant the role of symbols may be in the rite overall. At whichever point it takes place, because the word of God provides the basis and authority for all ministry, a copy of the *whole* Bible should be presented to deacons, presbyters, and bishops alike, and for the same reason its presentation should be the action of the presider rather than another minister.

The Welcome

In ancient practice, the newly ordained were greeted with a kiss by the bishop, their fellow clergy and the whole congregation, as a sign of their acceptance. At the least, the newly ordained should be presented to the whole congregation by the bishop, and the congregation might welcome them with signs such as applause or ululation, as culturally appropriate. Care should be taken lest the welcome overshadow other parts of the rite or become an occasion for focusing too closely on individuals and their families.

In some places it has become customary for the bishop to welcome newly ordained deacons and presbyters to their 'order,' when they are then greeted by other members of their order. In the case of deacons, however, their primary relationship is to the bishop and their congregation rather than to a diaconal 'college.' In the case of presbyters and bishops, other presbyters and bishops have just taken part in the laying on of hands, so only the welcome by the congregation as a whole is necessary at this point. However, if there is to be a welcome into a particular order, care should be taken not to portray a clericalized model of the church.

Celebrating at the Lord's Table

Some believe that the newly ordained should take an appropriate part in the remainder of the service, to exercise some aspects of their ministry. Examples would include deacons 'laying the table,' assisting with the distribution of communion, or giving the dismissal, and presbyters being visibly associated with the presider during the eucharistic prayer. Such practice is more readily done when there are few candidates. Where it takes place, it should not usurp the regular ministries of others and should involve all those who have been ordained, not just selected individuals.

Others believe that the ordination service should function as a ministry to the newly ordained. Following ordination, they should have opportunity to reflect and focus on the charism they have received from God, especially after reception of the communion. The initial exercise of their new ministries is better left to be done in the context within which they will minister. Since only the eucharistic parts of the service remain, an unbalanced view of diaconal and presbyteral ministry may be presented, and the false impression may be given that ministry is primarily liturgical.

In either case, the newly ordained should remain with their new order until sent out at the end of the service.

When a bishop is ordained in his or her own cathedral, it is appropriate that he or she be seated in the *cathedra* immediately after the Welcome and then preside at the eucharist.

Going out as God's People

The focus at the end of the service should be on sending forth the newly ordained to exercise their ministry in church and world, as part of a local baptismal community. The newly ordained might therefore appropriately be 'handed over' by the bishop to representatives of those among whom they will serve. As indicated earlier, this is also a very fitting context for the presentation of the Bible to the newly ordained.

If other secondary symbols of office are also to be presented at this time, this action by might be performed by ministers other than the presider. These should be items that the newly ordained would be able to take away with them, which might fittingly limit their number. Much will depend on local custom and culture. However, two considerations are paramount: first, the giving of secondary symbols must be subordinate to the primary aim of sending the newly ordained to minister with their community; and second, only the church's symbols should be used, and not personal gifts to the newly ordained from friends and family, which are more appropriately given in another context.

The pastoral staff is the central symbol which explicates the episcopal office. It might therefore be held by the new bishop during the final blessing and carried in procession. In some provinces, there is a custom of the retiring bishop presenting the staff.

C. *Other Points to be Considered*
Anointing

In some parts of the Communion, anointing the hands of a newly ordained presbyter with chrism, and anointing the head of a new bishop, have been introduced into ordination practice in imitation of Old Testament and medieval Western custom. While some would view this as a valuable link with baptismal anointing, others see it as opposed to a baptismal ecclesiology. When presbyters are anointed, it might be considered whether the anointing of the *head* would be a more appropriate symbol of their consecration to service.

17

Vesting

Vesting is not part of the act of ordination, but discloses the new standing of the ordained person. Care should therefore be taken that vesting does not in any sense distract attention from the centrality of the laying on of hands. The following places might be acceptable:

- candidates are vested before the service, entering already dressed for the ministry to which they have been called by the church, a practice adopted in the ancient Roman tradition;
- the newly ordained are vested after the conclusion of the prayer of ordination and the Welcome—not during or immediately after the prayer, where it would disrupt the integrity of the rite. This vesting need not be done in a place that is highly visible.

Other Symbols of Office

For bishops, some will wish to present a mitre, ring, and pectoral cross. This may be done in silence or with appropriate words.

For presbyters, a paten and chalice (communion plate and cup) are sometimes presented. These might be the set belonging to the local church. In cases where the new presbyters join the bishop at the table, these vessels may be brought to the table with the bread and wine at the eucharist, used in the distribution of communion, and then given to the presbyters when they are sent out at the end of the service.

For deacons, there is no generally accepted appropriate symbol of office.

The Ecclesiological Implications of the Setting for an Ordination

The choice of location for an ordination will emphasize a particular understanding of church and ministry. For example, the ordination of candidates in their diocesan cathedral may accent the universal dimension of ordained ministry; ordination within the parish where they will serve earths their ministry within the local community.

Occasionally there is good cause for a candidate to be ordained in a place other than their diocesan cathedral or parish church, perhaps in a different diocese or province. In order to make more evident the link between the candidate's ordination and the ministry of his or her local church, a rite of reception should be arranged at a suitable time soon after the ordination.

There is no compelling reason why episcopal ordinations should be restricted to feast days of apostles. The important principle is that they should take place in the presence and with the involvement of abundant representatives of the whole church.

The use of the normal presidential chair as the chair for the ordaining bishop links it with the church's normal eucharistic activity, especially if it is set in a position which declares that the bishop is presiding over the whole event, and not simply the ordination. For the ordination prayers and laying on of hands, the bishop need not be at the presidential chair.

The Place of the Family

The place of the family of the candidates at ordinations will vary from one culture to another, and needs to be considered with sensitivity and care. Faith and vocation have often been nourished and encouraged by the family of the candidate, who may wish them to be involved in some way in the liturgy. On occasions, however, the family may oppose or ignore the candidate's calling.

In many societies the extended family is central to community and church life, and failure to recognize this would detract considerably from the significance of the ordination service for the whole community. But does overemphasis on the family in the ordination service detract from ordination as an ecclesial event?

Important aspects to be considered will include where the family is placed for the occasion and possible provision for each candidate's family to receive communion together. In many cases the families will welcome such initiatives. However, in some cases candidates may not have close families or may come from families without faith. In such cases an overemphasis on family ties may be embarrassing and undesirable.

Appendix

The statement on ordination of the sixth International Anglican Liturgical Consultation held at the Church Divinity School of the Pacific, Berkeley, California needs to be seen in the light of the ecumenical movement in which liturgical renewal has played and continues to play a significant role. The deliberations of the Consultation were implicitly informed by the various multilateral and bilateral conversations in which the member provinces of the Anglican Communion have been involved. In addition to direct quotation from the World Council of Churches' document *Baptism, Eucharist and Ministry* of 1982, the participants authorized an appendix containing relevant references from recent Anglican bilateral conversations.

These references are grouped around five themes that emerge from the Berkeley Statement: (a) The primacy of a baptismal ecclesiology, (b) the ministry of the episcopate, (c) the ministry of the presbyterate, (d) the ministry of the diaconate, and (e) the act of ordination.

a) Baptismal Ecclesiology

In confessing the apostolic faith as a community, all baptized and believing Christians are the apostolic church and stand in the succession of apostolic faith. The apostolic ministry which was instituted by God through Jesus Christ in sending of the apostles is shared in varying ways by members of the whole body. (*Anglican-Lutheran International Conversations: The Report of the Conversations 1970–1972 authorized by the Lambeth Conference and the Lutheran World Federation*, London, UK: SPCK, 1973, para 75)

Together with other Churches, Anglicans and Lutherans are rediscovering the importance of the ministry of the whole People of God, the general priesthood of all baptized believers. This priesthood has its foundation in the unique priesthood of Jesus Christ and is given through baptism. Its members are called and sent by Christ and are equipped with the gifts of the Holy Spirit to fulfil their priestly task in everyday life as well as within the Christian community. They do this by offering themselves, their love and commitment in witnessing to Christ and serving others. In our largely secularized societies this witness and service of committed Christian lay people is more than ever required as an essential part of the missionary vocation of the church. (Anglican-Lutheran European Regional Commission. *Anglican-Lutheran Dialogue: The Report of the Anglican-Lutheran European Regional Commission, Helsinki, August-September 1982*, London, UK: SPCK, 1983, para 34)

The church lives in *koinonia* and is a community in which all members, lay or ordained, contribute their gifts to the life of the whole. (*Anglican-*

Lutheran Dialogue, 1983, para 48).

The church is an embodiment of God's final purpose for all human beings and for all creation because it is a body of actual men and women chosen by God to share through the Spirit in the life of Christ and so in his ministry in the world. (Anglican-Reformed International Commission, *God's Reign and Our Unity: The Report of the Anglican-Reformed International Commission 1981–1984: Woking, England, January 1984,* London, UK: SPCK, 1984; Edinburgh, UK: The Saint Andrew Press, 1984, para 30)

The rediscovery of a missionary perspective has been made possible by the experience of the world-wide church during the recent centuries of missionary expansion. This has helped us to enter again into the perspective of the New Testament, where the church is a small evangelizing community in a pagan society, ministry is primarily leadership in mission, baptism is commitment to that mission, and eucharist is the continued renewal of that commitment. (*God's Reign and Our Unity,* 1984, para 36)

It is to the whole church that the commission is given and it is to the whole church that the gift of the Spirit is made. The church as a whole is constituted by this act of sending and anointing...The primary ministry is that of the risen Christ himself, and we are enabled to participate in it by the power of the Spirit...This ministry is exercised by and through the entire membership of the church. Every member of the church, therefore, abiding in Christ, shares in this ministry. (*God's Reign and Our Unity,* 1984, para 74).

Every member of the church is an integral part of its witness and its mission; and every member has received a gift of the Holy Spirit so that the whole may flourish. (Anglican-Lutheran International Continuation Committee, *The Niagara Report: Report of the Anglican-Lutheran Consultation on Episcope, Niagara Falls, September 1987,* London, UK: Church House Publishing, 1988, para 17)

We believe that all members of the church are called to participate in its apostolic mission. All the baptized are therefore given various gifts and ministries by the Holy Spirit... This is the corporate priesthood of the whole people of God and the calling to ministry and service (1 Peter 2.5). (*Together in Mission and Ministry: The Porvoo Common Statement with Essays on Church and Ministry in Northern Europe,* London, UK: Church House Publishing, 1993, para 32.i)

Through baptism persons are initiated into the ministry of the whole church. Incumbent upon all the baptized is the exercise of *leitourgia, martyria,* and *diakonia.* (Anglican-Lutheran International Commission, *The Diaconate as Ecumenical Opportunity: The Hanover Report of the Anglican-Lutheran International Commission,* London, UK: Anglican Communion Publications, 1996, para 24)

b) Bishops

Episcope or oversight concerning the purity of apostolic doctrine, the ordination of ministries, and pastoral care of the church is inherent in the apostolic character of the church's life, mission, and ministry. (*Anglican-Lutheran International Conversations, 1973,* para 79)

This pastoral authority belongs primarily to the bishop, who is responsible for preserving and promoting the integrity of the koinonia in order to further the church's response to the Lordship of Christ and its commitment to mission… He does not, however, act alone. All those who have ministerial authority must recognize their mutual responsibility and interdependence. ('Authority in the Church I' in Anglican-Roman Catholic International Commission, *The Final Report: Windsor, September 1981* London, UK: SPCK, 1982; London, UK: Catholic Truth Society, 1982, para 5)

…episcope, *ie* the function of pastoral leadership, co-ordination and oversight. (*Anglican-Lutheran Dialogue 1982,* para 40)

…The local bishop can only perform his ministry: (1) in unity with his brother bishops, especially when meeting synodically; (2) in unity with his flock, both clergy and laity. In exercising the ministry of oversight he should pay heed to the prophetic and other gifts which Christ gives his people (Rom 12.6–8; Eph 4.11–12). (Anglican-Orthodox Joint Doctrinal Commission, *Anglican-Orthodox Dialogue: The Dublin Agreed Statement,* London, UK: SPCK, 1985, para 17)

It is the oversight or presiding ministry which constitutes the heart of the episcopal office, and that oversight is never to be viewed apart from the continuity of apostolic faith. (*The Niagara Report,* 1988, para 54)

Oversight of the church and its mission is the particular responsibility of the bishop. The bishop's office is one of service and communication within the community of believers and, together with the whole community, to the world. (*Together in Mission and Ministry,* 1993, para 43)

c) Presbyters/Priests

Presbyters are joined with the bishop in his oversight of the church and in the ministry of the word and the sacraments; they are given authority to preside at the eucharist and to pronounce absolution. ('Ministry and Ordination' in *The Final Report,* para 9)

The community needs ordained ministers, because the source of its life is Word and Sacrament, because it needs to be equipped for its witness and service (*Anglican-Lutheran Dialogue 1982,* para 37)

In their service, [ordained ministers] are related to the priesthood of Christ and accordingly also to the priesthood of all baptized believers…which they help to strengthen and build up through Word and Sacrament, their intercession and their pastoral guidance. In this sense ordained ministers in Anglican Churches and some Lutheran Churches are called priests. (*Anglican-*

Lutheran Dialogue 1982, para 37).

We recognize however that the word 'priest,' used of an ordained minister, has acquired overtones which render it unacceptable to many Christians. We would not in such circumstances expect the word to be universally used. We would, however, wish to insist that while the word may appropriately be used, other words, such as pastor, presbyter, minister, are no less appropriate. (*God's Reign and Our Unity*, 1984, para 79)

Those who may thus be called 'priests' exercise their priestly ministry neither apart from the priesthood of the whole body, nor by derivation from the priesthood of the whole body, but by virtue of their participation, in company with the whole body, in the priestly ministry of the risen Christ, and as leaders, examples and enablers for the priestly ministry of the whole body... (*God's Reign and Our Unity*, 1984, para 80)

d) Deacons

Deacons...are associated with bishops and presbyters in the ministry of word and sacrament, and assist in oversight. ('Ministry and Ordination' in *The Final Report 1981*, para 9)

A general description of diaconal ministers can be given: Diaconal ministers are called to be agents of the church in interpreting and meeting needs, hopes and concerns within church and society. (*The Diaconate as Ecumenical Opportunity*, 1996, para 48)

As a specific and focal form of a task to which all Christians are called, the service of one's neighbour, diaconal ministry should foster and bring to wider recognition the ministry of others, rather than making their ministries redundant or superfluous. The diaconal minister should lead and inspire the wider church in its service. (*The Diaconate as Ecumenical Opportunity*, 1996, para 56)

e) The Act of Ordination

Because ministry is in and for the community and because ordination is an act in which the whole church of God is involved, this prayer and laying on of hands take place within the context of the eucharist.. ('Ministry and Ordination' in *The Final Report 1981*, para 14)

It is God who calls, ordains, and sends the ministers of Word and Sacrament in the church. He does this through the whole people, acting by means of those who have been given authority so to act in the name of God and of the whole church. Ordination to the ministry gives authority to preach the gospel and administer the sacraments according to Christ's command and promise, for the purpose of the continuance of the apostolic life and mission of the church. Ordination includes the prayer of all the people and the laying on of hands of other ministers, especially of those who occupy a ministry of oversight and unity in the church (*Anglican-Lutheran International*

Conversations 1972, para 78).

In our traditions we hold that in the act of ordination the triune God, through the church, calls, blesses and sends the ministers of Word and Sacraments. They receive a special authority and responsibility from God in Christ and at the same time and by the same act they receive authority to minister from the whole People of God. (*Anglican-Lutheran Dialogue 1982*, para 36)

Ordination is the act which constitutes and acknowledges this special ministry of representation and leadership within the life of the church both locally and universally. In the act of ordination, the church in Christ prays to the Father to grant his Spirit to the one ordained for the office and work to which that person is called, accompanying the act with a sacramental sign which specifies by the imposition of hands the one for whom the prayer is made, and—in faith that the prayer is heard—commits to the person ordained the authority to act representatively for the universal church in the ways proper to that particular office. (*God's Reign and Our Unity: The Report of the Anglican-Reformed International Commission 1981–1984: Woking, England, January 1984*, para 80)

(Compiled by Richard G Leggett)

Present at the Consultation

Anthony Aarons, Alan Barthel, Tennyson Bogar, Molanga Botola, Paul Bradshaw, Perry Brohier, Robert Brooks, Colin Buchanan, Jean Campbell, Merwyn Castle, Christopher Cocksworth, George Connor, Bill Crockett, Ian D Darby, Keith Denison, Carol Doran, Ronald Dowling, Mark Earey, Richard Fabian, Kevin Flynn, Alec George, John Gibaut, Paul Gibson, Benjamin Gordon-Taylor, Donald Gray, Robert Gribben, Keith Griffiths, George Guiver, Jeremy Haselock, David Hebblethwaite, John W B Hill, David Holeton, Christopher Irvine, Bruce Jenneker, Joyce Karuri, John Hiromichi Kato, Richard Leggett, Trevor Lloyd, Cynara (Tessa) Mackenzie, Tomas Maddela, Gordon Maitland, Azad Marshall, Richard Cornish Martin, Brian Mayne, Ruth Meyers, Harold Miller, Ronald Miller, Boyd Morgan, Clayton Morris, Ishmael Mukuwanda, Gilly Myers, Martin Blaise Nyaboho, Nelson Nyumbe, Martin Nzaramba, Juan Oliver, Sue Parks, Ian Paton, William Petersen, Isaac Mar Philoxenos, Ellison Pogo, Alphege Rakotovao, Alfred Reid, Anderson Saefoa, Vincent Shamo, John Simalenga, Susan Marie Smith , Bryan Spinks, David Stancliffe, Gillian Varcoe, Louis Weil, Carol Wilkinson, John Masato Yoshida, Ian Young.